My Weekly Reader

My Weekly Reader
PICTURE WORD BOOK

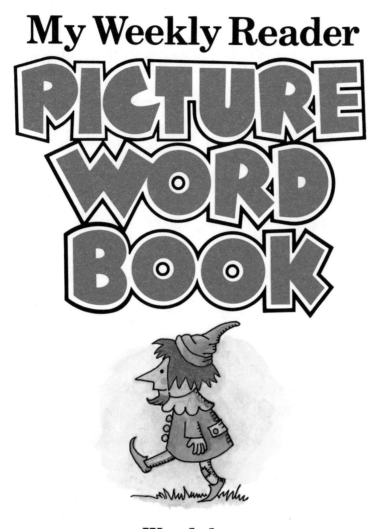

**Words by
Adelaide Holl**

**Pictures by
Alfred Perry**

GROSSET & DUNLAP
Publishers • New York

A Word to Parents and Teachers

My Weekly Reader Picture Word Book is designed to introduce the young child to the pleasures of the printed page—to the fun of words and pictures. It provides early exposure to a broad vocabulary, leading to the development of the language and thinking skills that will be needed in the learning of reading.

The words have been carefully selected to include those commonly used in the child's everyday vocabulary, words a child frequently hears and understands (though he may not use them fluently), and a number of new words for vocabulary enrichment.

Words are presented, not in isolation, but in meaningful groups—people, animals, toys, vehicles, seasons, holidays, and so on. All words are clearly defined in pictures with plenty of color and action, and the kind of humor that will help to hold the youngster's attention. Every page offers opportunities for active participation by the child. There are word games and puzzles, riddles and rhymes, stories in picture sequence, and stories with rebuses. Once a concept has been introduced, it is continually reinforced, through stories and pictures, as the book moves along.

As a child becomes involved in the stories and games, he is not only having fun but he is learning to think, to make choices, to see relationships, to understand cause and effect, to recognize logical sequence, to make inferences and judgments, to predict outcomes, and to draw conclusions. He is enlarging his knowledge of basic concepts—color, number, size, shape and dimension, form, position, and detail. He is gaining valuable experience with oral language in naming, describing, discussing, and story telling. As he begins to associate a printed symbol (the word) with the idea it represents (the picture) he is laying foundations for reading.

For the child's special enjoyment, a central character appears throughout the book. He is a little monkey named JoJo, who is lively, inquisitive, prankish, and usually involved in a comical situation. With JoJo's amusing help, the young child will learn much that he needs to know, and will have fun along the way.

—*Adelaide Holl*

ISBN: 0-88375-105-4 (Xerox Education Publications Edition)

ISBN: 0-448-13276-1 (Grosset & Dunlap Library Edition)

ISBN: 0-448-11783-5 (Grosset & Dunlap Trade Edition)

6

men

girl baby boys

man

KEEP OFF THE GRASS

children

boy

ICE CREAM

Make up names for the people in the picture. Talk about the fun everyone is having in the park.

7

Families

father

mother

grandfather

grandmother

daughter

son

Mommy Mouse

Daddy Mouse

baby mice

husband and wife

win sisters

brother and sister

baby brother

Name the members of *your* family. Tell about a time *you* had fun at a picnic.

9

Workers

teachers

nurse

police officers

veterinarian

pilot   stewardess

secretary

astronaut

construction workers

doorman

TV announcer

cowboy

barber

farmer

soldier   **sailor**

fireman

clown

Name the workers. Tell about the useful work each one does. How is each of these workers helpful to you?

11

doctors   **hairdresser**   **dancers**

actor   **actress**   **salesman**

business man   **business woman**   **storekeeper**   **scientists**

12

acrobats

mailman

dentist

musicians

mechanic

author

artists

What would you like to be when you grow up?

13

Who Am I?

I work in a classroom.
I help children learn to read and
    write.

Who am I?

an author   **a teacher**

I help put up buildings.
I wear a hard hat.

Who am I?

a construction worker   **a doorman**

I wear a space suit.
I travel far in my rocket ship.

Who am I?

an airplane pilot   **an astronaut**

I live in the country.
I grow food for hungry people.

Who am I?

a storekeeper   **a farmer**

You may see me on the stage.
You may see me in a movie or
    on TV.

Who am I?

an actress   **a barber**

I work on a ranch out west.
I help round up cattle.

Who am I?

a sailor   **a cowboy**

I am helpful when you take a trip
in an airplane.
Sometimes I serve your dinner.

Who am I?

an airplane pilot   **a stewardess**

I wear a uniform and a shiny badge.
I help people in trouble.
I help keep the city safe.

Who am I?

a police officer   **a doctor**

My patients are animals.
I help them when they are sick.
I keep people's pets well.

Who am I?

a nurse   **a veterinarian**

I take care of all kinds of machines.
I repair things that are broken.
Sometimes I work on cars and
    trucks.
Who am I?

a storekeeper   **a mechanic**

I dress in white.
I work with a doctor.
I help care for sick people.

Who am I?

a hairdresser   **a nurse**

I work in a circus.
I wear funny clothes.
I make people laugh.

Who am I?

a musician   **a clown**

Can you answer these riddles?
The pictures will help you.

15

Storybook People

giant's castle

elf

giant

Little Miss Bear

Mrs. Bear

Mr. Bear

brownie

Prince   Princess

Queen   King

three little pigs

monster

haunted house

ghost

wizard

enchanted forest

fairy

dwarfs

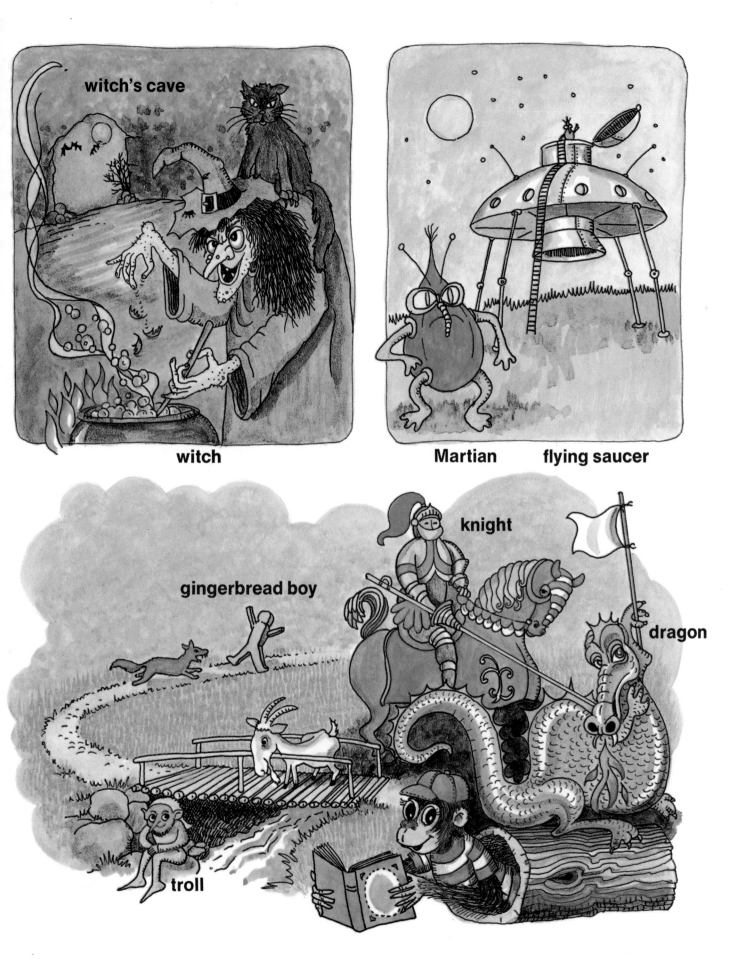

witch's cave

witch

Martian   flying saucer

knight

gingerbread boy

dragon

troll

The Royal Birthday Party

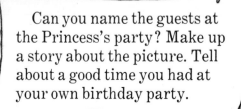

Can you name the guests at the Princess's party? Make up a story about the picture. Tell about a good time you had at your own birthday party.

21

Parts of the Body

head

neck

shoulder

arm

elbow

hand

fingernail

finger

hip

heel

ankle

foot

toe

knee

chest

wrist

stomach

waist

leg

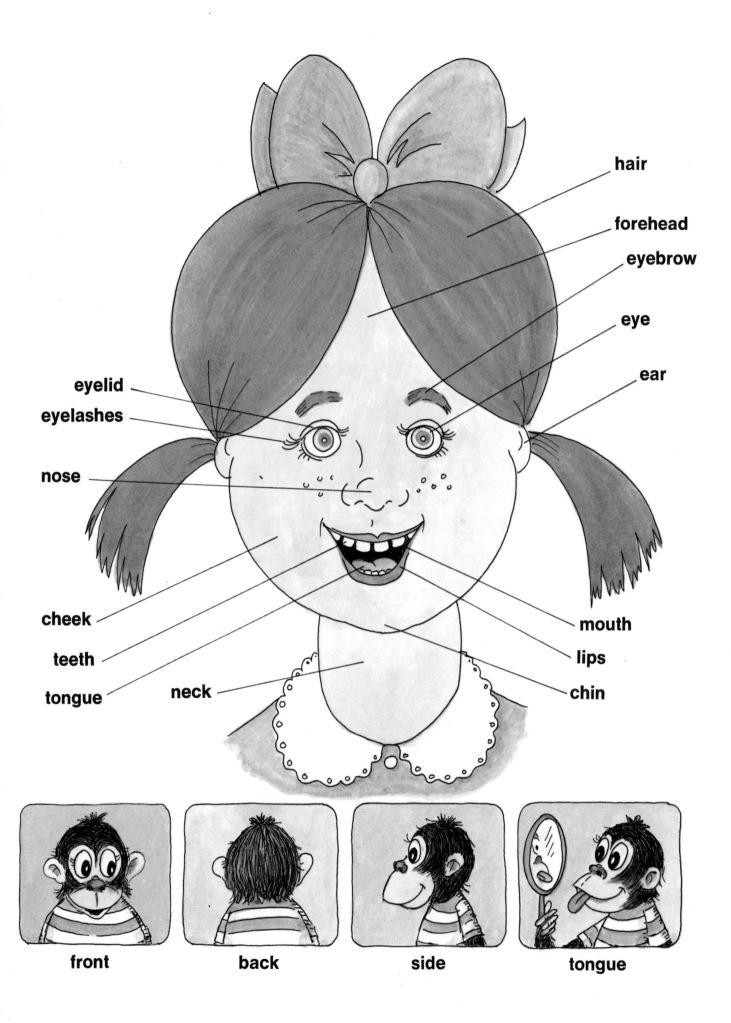

hair

forehead

eyebrow

eye

ear

eyelid

eyelashes

nose

cheek

teeth

tongue

mouth

lips

chin

neck

front

back

side

tongue

23

Colors

red   blue   yellow   green   orange   purple

red

blue

yellow

green

orange

purple

Yellow

pink   gray   brown   black   white   tan

pink   gray   brown

black   white   tan

The Little Polka Dot Bear

Bruno Bear was a small brown cub. He lived with Mother Bear and Little Sister Bear in a cave at the bottom of a hill. Bruno and Little Sister played happily at the edge of a little green woods near the cave. But their mother kept telling them again and again, "Don't ever go up that hill! Do you see that little white house? Do you see that big red barn? People live up there. Bears are not safe around people."

Sometimes Bruno was naughty. He didn't listen to his mother. So one day, he became so curious about people that he decided to go up the hill and look around.

He climbed and climbed all the way to the top. There sat the big red barn. Quietly Bruno crept inside.

Now the farmer who lived in the little white house had been painting that day. He had been painting walls, and floors, and windows, and fences. He had left his paint cans and paint brushes in a corner of the barn.

Bruno was curious. He looked, and sniffed, and poked at the paint cans. "I wonder if these are people," he said to himself. He pushed off the can lids and peered inside. "If these are people, they are very pretty. And I'm not afraid of them at all."

He dipped in his nose and his paws. He dipped in his ears and his tail. He spilled the paint. He splashed it all about. He even rolled in it. Before long, he was not a little brown bear anymore. He was a little polka dot bear. His left ear was blue. His right ear was red. He had one green paw, one pink paw, one yellow paw, and one that was a lovely orange. His stubby little tail was a beautiful bright purple. And all over his soft, brown fur there were spots and drops and polka dots of every color.

Just when he was having the most fun, he heard somebody coming. He was frightened. He ran and ran as fast as he could go, out the door and down the hill toward home.

Little Sister saw him coming. She called out in a frightened voice, "Mommy! Mommy! There's a terrible-looking thing coming down the hill. It's a polka dot monster!"

"Come inside quickly," cried her mother. She closed the door with a bang.

Bruno pounded at the door. "Let me in! Let me in!" he begged.

But a voice from inside said, "Go away, you horrible monster!"

Bruno pounded again and again, but it was no use. At last, he crept away and crawled under a bush. He was cold. He was hungry. He was lonely. He was also very tired, and pretty soon he fell fast asleep.

During the night, it rained and rained and rained. When Bruno woke up in the morning, he was not only cold, and hungry, and lonely, he was also very wet.

Sadly he looked around. "I guess Mother Bear and Little Sister don't know me," he said to himself. "Maybe I can never go home again." He thought about juicy red berries and sweet golden honey for breakfast. A tear ran down his nose and splashed into a puddle on the ground.

Bruno looked down. There, in a puddle of rainwater, he suddenly saw his own reflection. "Ohhhh, Ohhhh!" he cried. He jumped up and down with excitement. He was no longer a little polka dot bear. He looked just like a small brown bear cub once more. The rain had washed off all the paint.

Bruno stared at his reflection for a moment. He said to himself, "I'll never, never go up the hill again!"

Then, with a happy little bear growl, he went running home to his mother.

If you have paper and colored crayons, you might like to draw your own picture of the little polka dot bear.

Clothes and Things

stockings, socks

umbrellas, raincoats, rain hats

skirts

sweaters

bathing suits

belts, handkerchiefs, scarfs

pants, jeans

shorts, panties, petticoats

handbags, shoulder bags

T-shirts

shoes, boots, slippers, sneakers

jackets   coats

gloves, mittens

bathrobes, pajamas

dresses

shirts, blouses

hats

caps

too big

too small

just right

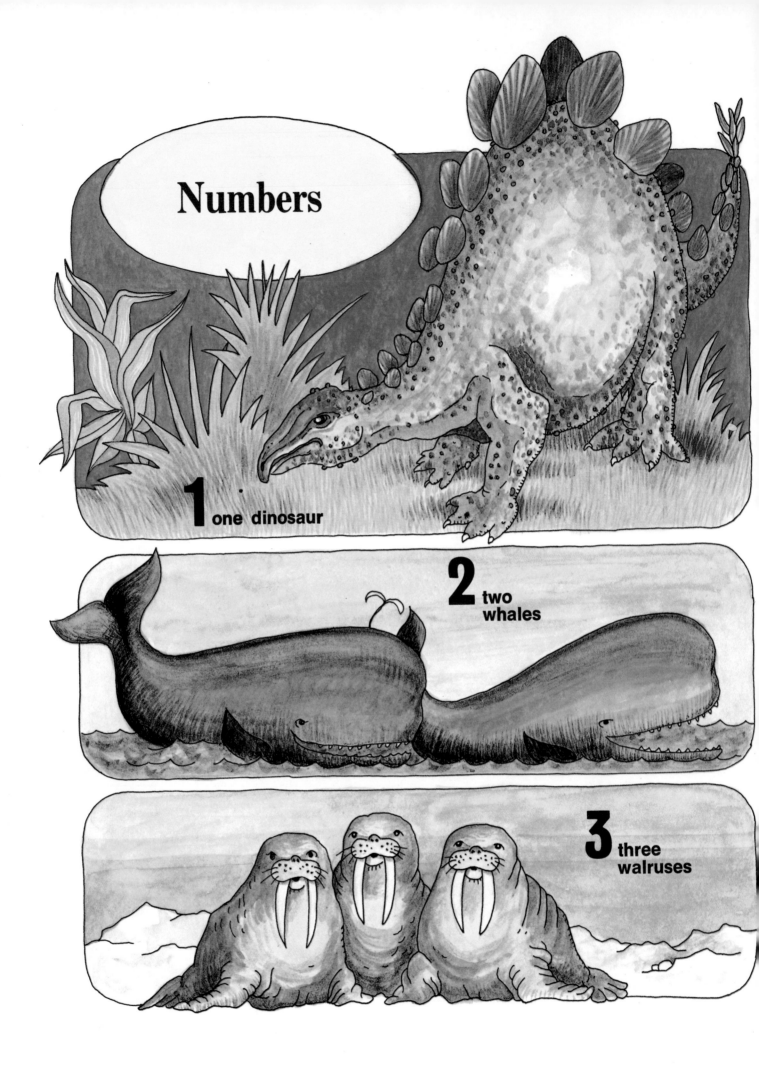

Numbers

1 one dinosaur

2 two whales

3 three walruses

4 four foxes

5 five bighorn sheep

6 six burros

7 seven armadillos

8 eight prairie dogs

9 nine chipmunks

10 ten moles

Who Is Prettiest?

The forest animals were having a beauty contest. They were going to choose the prettiest animal in the forest. The judges were **3** owls.

"I'm the prettiest!" boasted Raccoon. "Look at the **7** beautiful black rings around my tail!"

"You're wrong," said Rabbit. "I have **2** beautiful long ears and **4** beautiful, quick-hopping legs."

"Who needs **4** legs?" said Robin. "I have only **2** legs, and they are much prettier than yours."

Ladybug laughed. "Everyone should have **6** legs like me. That's what is really beautiful."

"Oh, no!" spoke up Spider. "Anyone who wants to be really beautiful has to have **8** legs just like my pretty ones."

There were **5** little green snakes in the grass. One snake said, "That's silly! Look at us! We haven't any legs at all. See how pretty we are!"

"Snake is right," said **9** little earthworms, poking their heads out of the ground. "The prettiest animals have no legs at all."

"That's true," spoke up a small caterpillar. "The most beautiful animal in the forest has no legs, and it has a lovely green coat with **10** black stripes. That makes me a winner!"

Just then, **1** of the owls called down to the others. "The judges have made up their minds. Nobody wins, and nobody loses," he said. "You are all beautiful in your own special way."

Help read the story. Someone else can read the words, and you can read the numbers.

The Race

Hurry! Come watch
This exciting race!
Rabbit's blue car
Is in first place.

Second in line
Is a big red truck.
And look who is driving!
It's a yellow duck.

Swift as an arrow,
     And coming in third,
Are a little gray car
     And a dodo bird.

A black-and-white racer
     Is fourth in line.
The driver's a funny
     Fat porcupine.

JoJo is fifth.
     He's just rounding the bend.
And who is that
     At the very end?

It's Pinky Pig
     And his car of green.
He has run out
     Of gasoline.

fourth

third

second

The Sillies

These are the Sillies.

Silly Millie is going to a party.

Silly Billy is going swimming.

Silly Billy is watching TV.

Silly Millie is making a snowman.

Silly Millie   Silly Billy

The Sillies are always doing funny things.
Look at the pictures.
Can you find the silly things they are doing?

Silly Millie is sending party invitations.

Silly Billy is proud of his new clothes.

Silly Billy is riding on his pony

Silly Millie and Silly Billy are
getting ready for Valentine's Day.

Pets

4 little kittens   **mother cat**

canary

2 parakeets

2 bunnies

2 guinea pigs

2 little puppies   **turtle**   **mother dog**

5 white mice   **3 goldfish**

hamster   **3 gerbils**

Choose a pet
you would
like to own.

39

Andy, the Animal Sitter

Andy wanted to make some money to buy a football. "My big sister gets paid for baby-sitting," thought Andy. "I'll bet I could get paid for animal-sitting."

He made a sign and put it up on the shed in the backyard.

It wasn't long before Andy began to have customers. Mrs. Martin stopped to leave her little gray poodle. "I'm going shopping," she said. "If I leave Fifi alone, she chews up slippers and rugs."

Mrs. McFeeney brought over a baby kitten. "I just got her yesterday," said Mrs. McFeeney. "She keeps crying for her mother. You play with her for a while, Andy. I'm busy."

A new family was moving in next door. The lady brought over a big green parrot. "Do you mind watching Polly while I unpack things?" she asked. "The noise and excitement make her nervous."

Janie was next. She stopped to leave her gray mice. "My grandmother is visiting us today," said Janie, "and she's real scared of mice. I'll pick them up tonight after she goes home."

Mary Jo brought over a fat hen in a box. "This is the baby chick I got for Easter," she said, "only she isn't a baby chick anymore. Will you keep her till my Dad makes a bigger pen for her?"

Mrs. Stevens left a bowl of gold fish. "I'm painting the walls," she told Andy, "and paint makes my pretty little goldfish sick. The poor darlings!"

Andy's friend Bob came over with a big blacksnake in a cardboard box. "I just caught him today," said Bob. "I don't want my mom to see him till I build him a good, tight cage."

Mr. Todd from across the street came to leave a big, furry tomcat. "He's a present for Suzy's birthday. I don't want her to know she's getting a cat until dinnertime tonight," explained Mr. Todd.

Andy had a very busy day. He had an exciting day.

He had lots of trouble too.

The [cat] tried to eat the [mice].

He tried to eat the [fish].

He pulled tail feathers out of the [parrot].

The [parakeet] got mad and bit the [poodle].

The [poodle] got mad and chased the [cat].

The [chicken] laid an egg and the [snake] ate it.

The [snake] got loose and slithered around the shed.

He scared the other animals half to death.

The [poodle] yelped and the [cat] mewed.

The [chicken] cackled and the [mice] squeaked.

The [parrot] squawked and the [cat] snarled.

And the [snake] hissed back at all of them.

Andy was a wreck when the day was over. But he had made a lot of money.

"Oh, boy!" said Andy. "Now I can get a football! But first I have one more thing to do!'"

He took down the sign that said

ANIMAL
SITTER
25 CENTS
AN HOUR

and he put up a new sign that said

LAWNS
MOWED
50 CENTS
AN HOUR

Then he took his money and ran off to the store.

You can help read the story. Someone else can read the words, and you can read the pictures.

Farm Animals

horse

colt

cow

geese

goslings

pony

farm dog

lamb

she[ep]

calf

goat

kid

turk[ey]

duck

ducklings

42

little bat

wren

barn owl

rooster

donkey

eggs

piglets

pig

farm cat

hen

barn mice

chicks

43

Woodland Animals

wolf

raccoon

the opossum family

gray squirrel

big mother bear   little bear cubs   red fox

the rabbit family

chipmunk

woodchuck

skunk

mole

beaver

field mouse

field mice

porcupine

mother deer   **fawn**   **father deer**

Make up a story about the picture. Give your story a name.

47

Zoo Animals

ape

grizzly bear and cubs

monkeys

rhinoceros

llamas

zebra

penguins

seal

polar bear

giant panda

giant anteater

red fox

elephant

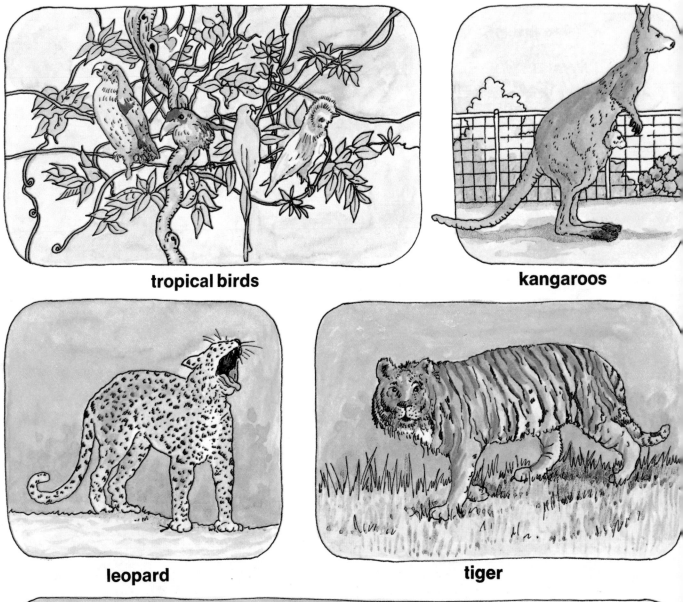

tropical birds

kangaroos

leopard

tiger

lion family

koala

camel

bison

snake

hippopotamus

51

Birds

wild geese

gulls

vulture

bald eagle

pelican

swan

sparrow

robin

bluebird

pigeon

woodpecker

goldfinch

wild ducks

great blue heron

53

penguins

owl

ring-necked pheasant

cactus wren

hawk

ostrich

peacock

cardinals

meadowlark

crow

roadrunner

hummingbird

Baltimore oriole

flamingo

55

Animals With Scales

American chameleon

garter snake

coral snake

leatherback turtle

mud turtle

turtle eggs

crocodile

horned lizard

iguana

alligator

baby alligator

56

Land and Water Animals

spotted salamander

green salamander

mud puppy

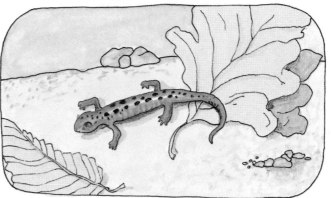

red-spotted newt

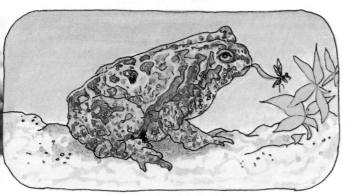

garden toad

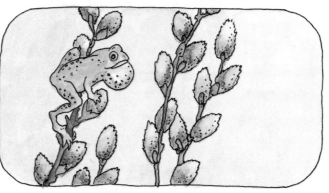

spring peeper

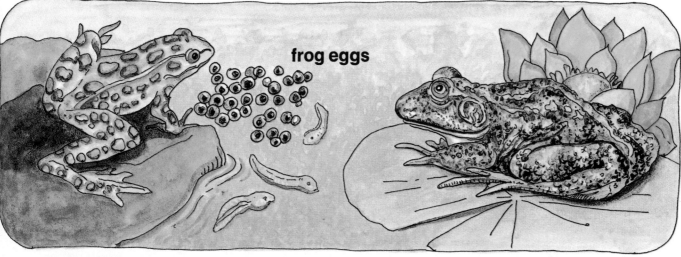

frog eggs

leopard frog   tadpoles   bullfrog

Insects, Spiders, and Worms

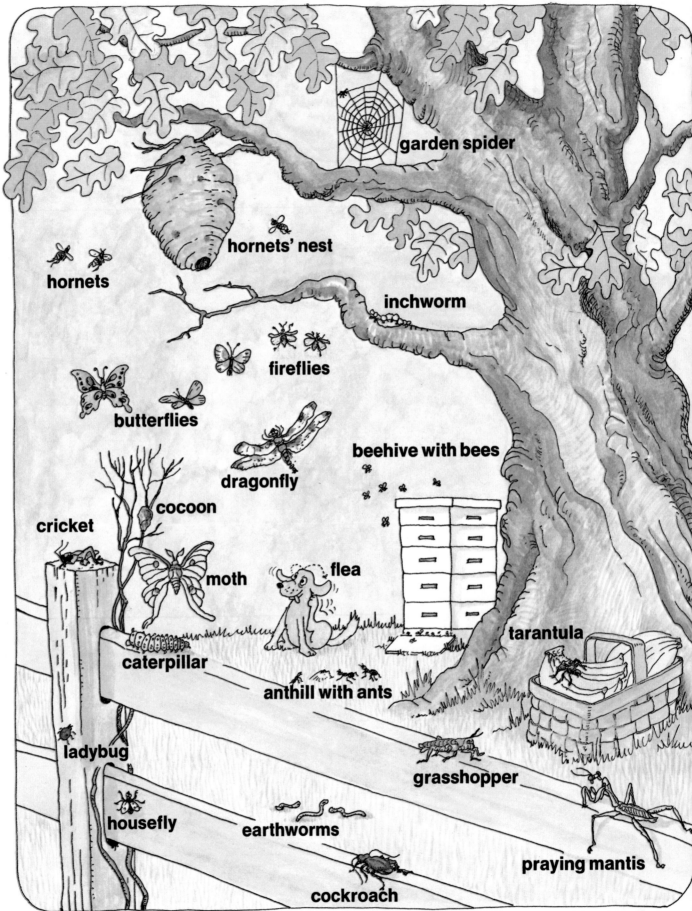

garden spider

hornets' nest

hornets

inchworm

fireflies

butterflies

dragonfly

beehive with bees

cocoon

cricket

moth

flea

tarantula

caterpillar

anthill with ants

ladybug

grasshopper

housefly

earthworms

praying mantis

cockroach

Water Animals

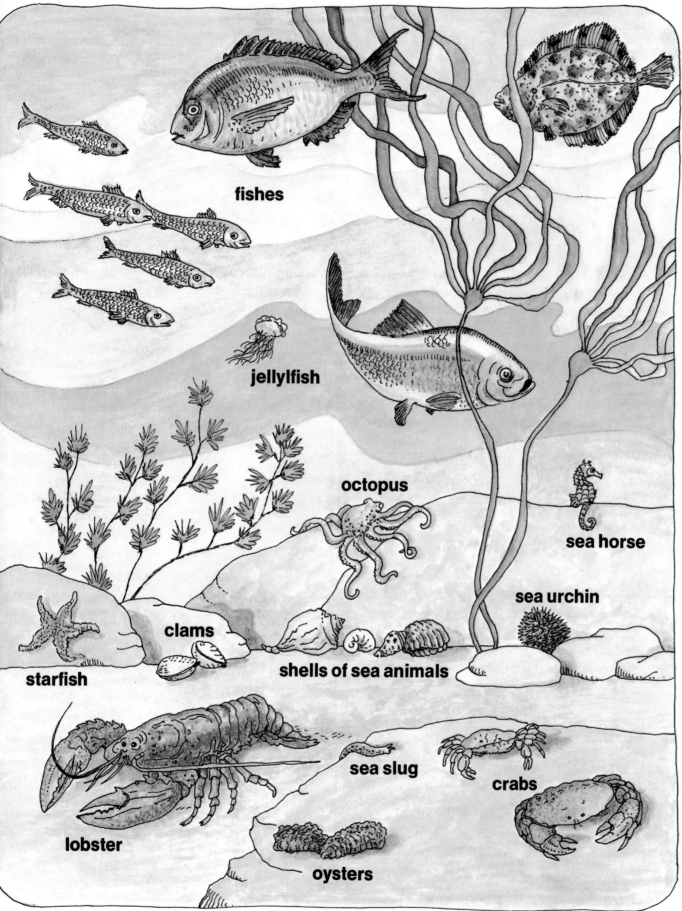

fishes

jellyfish

octopus

sea horse

sea urchin

starfish

clams

shells of sea animals

sea slug

crabs

lobster

oysters

Animal Riddles

I live in a tree.
I have a long, bushy tail.
I like to eat nuts.
My name is

owl   **squirrel**

I am yellow and black.
I can fly.
I can sing.
My name is

butterfly   **goldfinch**

I live on a farm.
I lay eggs.
My babies are called chicks.
My name is

hen   **duck**

I am black.
I have eight legs.
I spin silky thread.
My name is

spider   **ant**

I am beautifully colored.
I can fly.
I was once a caterpillar.
My name is

bluebird   **butterfly**

I am green and black.
I live in a pond.
Once I was a tadpole.
My name is

frog   **grasshopper**

60

I fly from flower to flower.
I make delicious honey.
I live in a hive.
My name is

hornet   **bee**

I am a bird but I cannot fly.
I live where it is very cold.
I am black and white.
My name is

penguin   **giant panda**

I am small and brown.
I hang upside down to sleep.
I have wings but I am not a bird.
My name is

moth   **bat**

I am small.
I have feathers.
I feed on flower nectar.
My name is

hummingbird honeybee

I lay eggs but I am not a bird.
I have a shell on my back.
I move very slowly.
My name is

turtle   **clam**

I have scales.
I have fins.
I cannot live out of water.
My name is

fish   **tadpole**

The Everything Tree

In a faraway land
   On the Island of Quee,
There's a wonderful plant
   Called The Everything Tree.

On its wide-spreading branches
   Grow all sorts of things—
Thimbles, and thumbtacks,
   And scissors, and strings,

Clothespins, safety pins,
   Needles, and nails,
Pencils, and paper,
   And pitchers, and pails.

From all over the world,
   People come just to see
The strange things that grow
   On The Everything Tree.

Can you name all the things that grow on this wonderful tree? Can you tell how people use them?

63

Sizes

big

little

huge

tiny

large

small

tall

short

long

short

long tail

short tail

SCOLOSAURUS   GORGOSAURUS   CAMARUSAURUS

big   bigger   biggest

small   smaller   smallest

The rat is larger than the mouse.

The mouse is smaller than the rat.

all the same size

many different sizes

too big   too small   just the right size

Miss Mouse's Cake

Little Miss Mouse was making a cake. She was just pouring the batter into a pan when up hopped her friend Rabbit.

"What a tiny cake!" said Rabbit. "How much flour did you use?"

"A cupful," Miss Mouse told him.

"That isn't nearly enough," said Rabbit. "You should have used a bowl full."

And away hopped Rabbit into the bushes.

Miss Mouse threw out the cake and mixed another one. She put in a bowl full of flour. She was just getting ready to pop the cake into the oven when up waddled her friend Bear.

"That's a fine cake," said Bear, "but it is awfully small. How much flour did you use?"

"A bowl full," said Miss Mouse.

"No wonder it's so little!" said Bear. "You should have used a bucket full."

And away Bear waddled into the woods.

Miss Mouse threw away the cake and mixed another one. She put in a bucket full of flour. She was just setting the cake in the oven when up lumbered her friend Elephant.

"That's not a very big cake," said Elephant. "You ought to make a bigger one. How much flour did you use?"

"A bucket full," said Miss Mouse.

66

"No wonder!" exclaimed Elephant. "You should have used a tub full."

And away lumbered Elephant into the forest.

Miss Mouse threw away the cake and mixed another one. She put in a tub full of flour. Then she shoved the cake into the oven.

In a little while the cake began to rise. It rose higher and higher. It grew bigger and bigger. When it was done, it was the biggest cake Miss Mouse had ever seen.

She stared at it in surprise. "What a huge cake for a tiny mouse!" she exclaimed. "I can't possibly eat all that by myself. I guess I'll have to have a tea party." And she did!

Shapes

circles

squares

triangles

rectangles

hearts

diamonds

stars

ovals

Shapes All Around Us

Can you name all the things pictured on this page? Can you tell the shape of each one?

Outside JoJo's House

tree

fence

gate

swing

window box

door

doorbell

awnin

mailbox

front walk

grassy lawn

chimney

roof

vines

bird feeder

porch

window

bushes

steps

flower bed

birdbath

Do you live in a house or an apartment? In what ways is your home like JoJo's? How is it different?

Inside
JoJo's House

bedroom

lamp

mirror

crib

dresser

stool

rug

living room

bookcase

curtains

picture

lamp

sofa

table

tel-

magazine

72

bathroom

medicine cabinet

soap

washcloth

towel

shower

washbowl

toilet

closet

pillow

bathtub

blanket

bed

bath mat

cupboards

kitchen

refrigerator

calendar

clock

sink

telephone

stove

table

chair

fireplace

Name the rooms in your home. How is your furniture like JoJo's? How is it different?

73

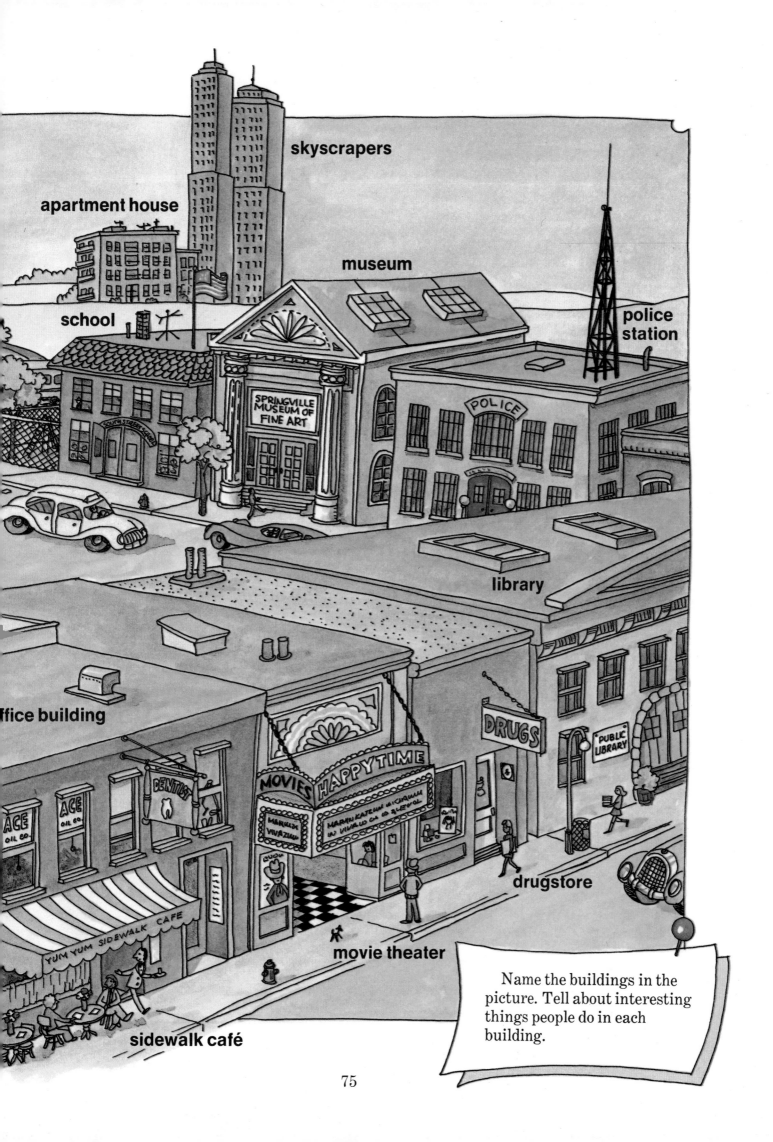

apartment house

skyscrapers

museum

police station

school

SPRINGVILLE MUSEUM OF FINE ART

POLICE

library

office building

DRUGS

PUBLIC LIBRARY

DENTIST

MOVIES HAPPYTIME

ACE OIL CO.

ACE OIL CO.

drugstore

YUM YUM SIDEWALK CAFE

movie theater

sidewalk café

Name the buildings in the picture. Tell about interesting things people do in each building.

75

bananas

pineapples

grapefruit

blueberries

avacados

cantaloupes

cherries

strawberries

grapes

oranges

lemons

nectarines

plums

apples

Name the fruits at the fruit stand. Which ones have you tasted? Which ones do you like best?

Tell about times you have helped do the shopping at a supermarket.

What Do You Like for Breakfast?

Name the foods in the picture. Which do you like best for breakfast? Tell how your favorite foods taste.

What Do You Like for Lunch?

Choose your favorite lunch from the foods in this picture.

80

What Do You Like for Dinner?

Pretend you are having dinner at a restaurant. You are going to order your dinner from a menu. Choose the foods you wish to order.

What Do You Like for Dessert?

Choose some desserts you like best from these pictures.

JoJo's Picture Gallery

Ostrich

Zebra

Circles

Five Baby Chicks

Little Red Wagon

Happy Princess

Fruit Basket

Jolly Fat Clown

Sailboat

Garden Spider

Skyscraper

The Magic Dragon

Lion Cub

Ten Little Turtles

The Rabbit Family

The Apple Tree

JoJo is having an exhibit of his paintings. Sometimes JoJo makes mistakes in his pictures. Can you find the mistakes?

Things That Go on Land

horse and wagon

fire engine

school bus

taxi

gasoline truck

dump truck

sanitation truck

ambulance

police car

city bus

tow truck

delivery truck

Can you name these vehicles? Can you tell how each one is useful?

More Things That Go on Land

fire chief's car

bicycle

motorcycle

utility truck

camper

train

mail truck

station wagon

jeep

snowmobile

MOVERS

trailer truck

cars

Name the vehicles. Which have you had a ride in? Which would you like to ride?

Things That Go in Water

raft

rowboat

canoe

sailboat

motorboat

houseboat

ferryboat

freighter   **submarine**

barge   **yacht**

fishing trawler

tugboats   **ocean liner**

Which of these boats have you seen? Which have you traveled in? Which would you like to travel in?

Things That Go in the Air

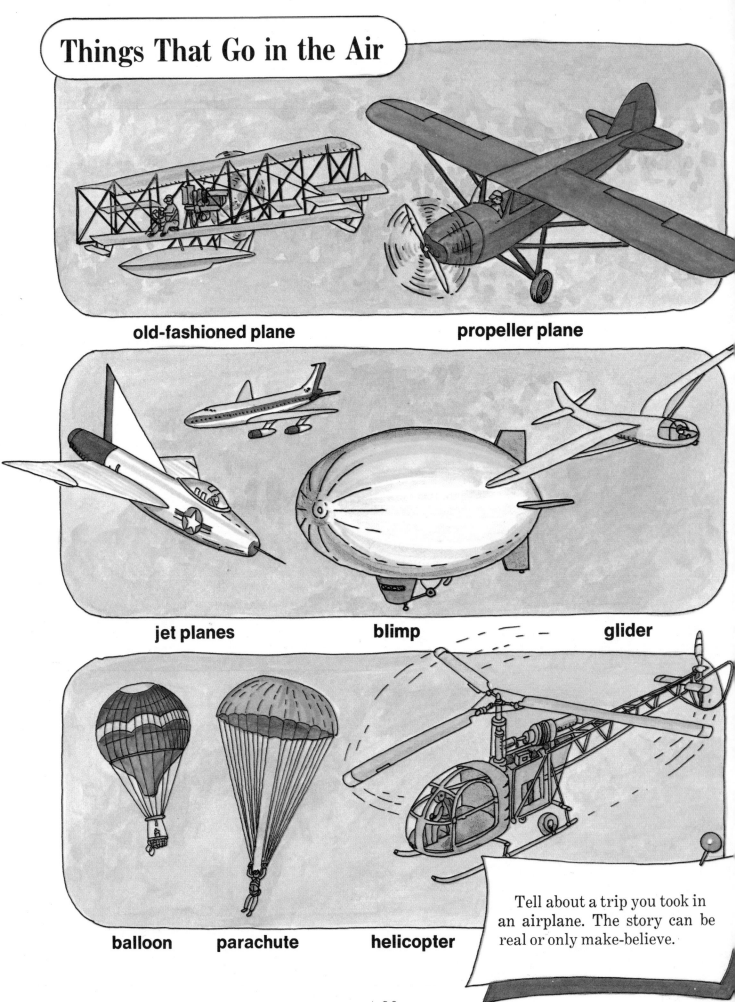

old-fashioned plane **propeller plane**

jet planes **blimp** **glider**

balloon **parachute** **helicopter**

Tell about a trip you took in an airplane. The story can be real or only make-believe.

90

Things That Go in Space

satellites　　　　　**space capsule**

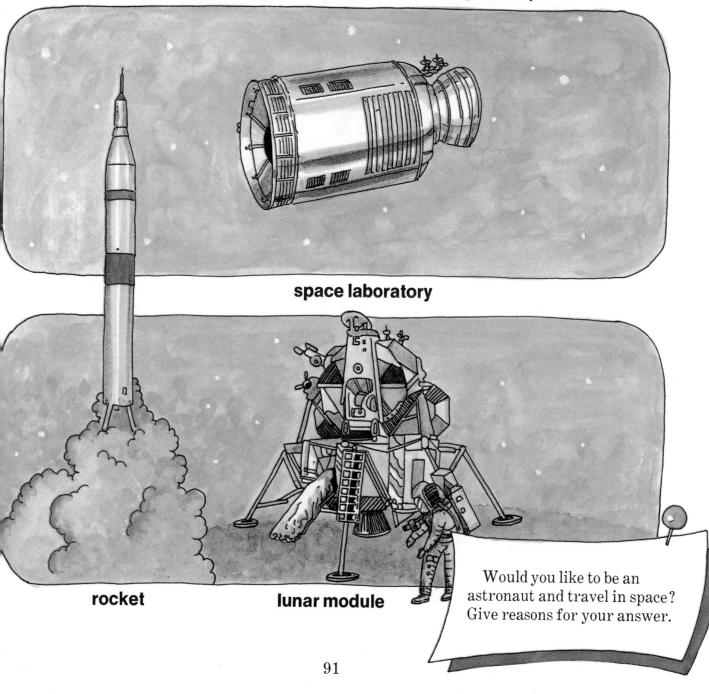

space laboratory

rocket　　　　**lunar module**

Would you like to be an astronaut and travel in space? Give reasons for your answer.

Big Machines

tractor

earth mover

roller

grader

bulldozer

crane

computer

Which of these big machines would you like to operate? Tell how you would use each one.

Little Machines

lawn mower　　sewing machine　　electric fan　　vacuum cleaner

tape recorder　　　movie projector　　iron　　　blender

typewriter

record player　　　　toaster

What are some little machines you have at your house? What kind of work does each one do?

93

Signs and
Signals

Go for a walk and look for all kinds of signs near your house.

At the Department Store

LOST AND FOUND

DOWN ESCALATOR

CASHIER▼

ASK
about
our
GIFT
WRAP

FIRE HOSE

PULL

Rest Rooms

WOMEN

MEN

PUSH

FIRE
ESCAPE

EMERGENCY

SNACK
BAR

Tell about a time you went
shopping in a big store.

In the Toy Store

Choose some toys you would
like to buy in the toy store. Tell
exactly what each one looks
like.

JoJo's Busy Week

Sunday

Monday

Tuesday

Wednesday

Thursday

Friday

Saturday

Make up a story about JoJo's busy week and about the party he had. The pictures will help you.

April

May

June

October

November

December

At School

clock

1 2 3 4 5 6 7 8 9 10 11 12 13 14 15 16 17 18 19 20

A B C D E F G H I J K L M N O P Q R S T

plants

chalkboard

teacher's aide

BULLETIN

calendar

chalk

eraser

science table

aquarium

magnet

fish

table

pupils

easel

rocks

shells

turtle

sandbox

globe of the world

flag

principal

boards

plane

hammer

books

saw

vise

workbench

drill

NAILS

chair

stool

screwdriver

teacher

blocks

pet

Y Z

107

FARM MARKET

Indian corn

scales

farmer

gourds

cider

apples

baskets

customer

How does the picture show that it is fall? Does autumn look like this where you live? How is your autumn like the picture? How is it different?

bare trees

evergreen trees

snowshoes

snowball fight

snowdrift

icicles

snowman

Have you ever had fun in the snow? If you have, tell about it.

109

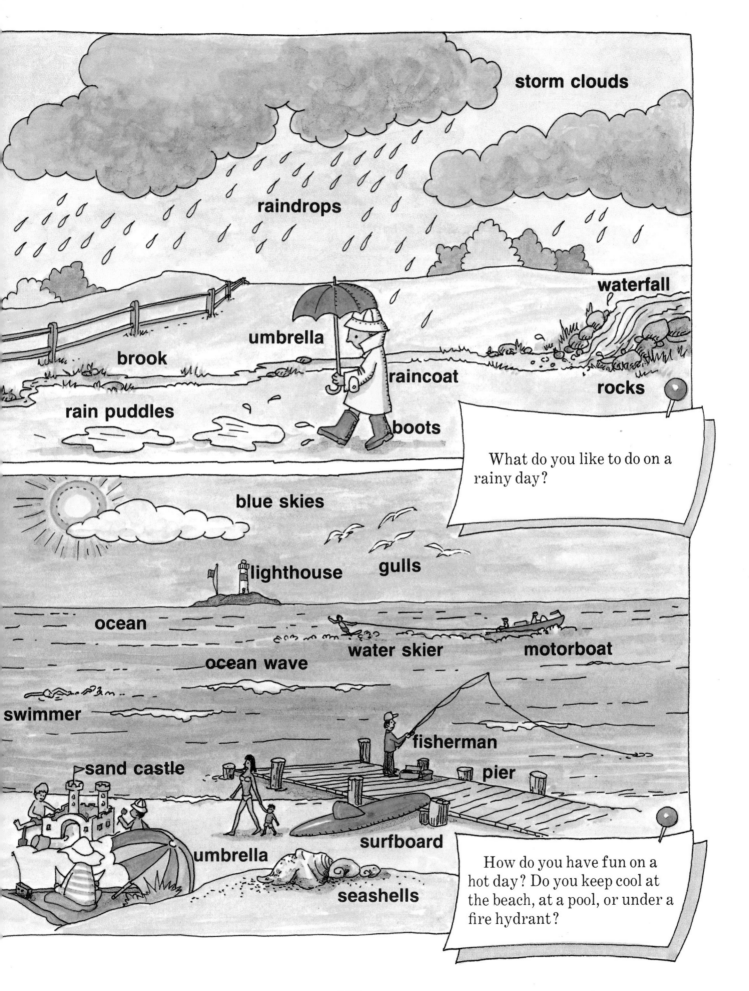

storm clouds

raindrops

waterfall

umbrella

brook

raincoat

rocks

rain puddles

boots

What do you like to do on a rainy day?

blue skies

lighthouse

gulls

ocean

water skier

motorboat

ocean wave

swimmer

fisherman

sand castle

pier

umbrella

surfboard

seashells

How do you have fun on a hot day? Do you keep cool at the beach, at a pool, or under a fire hydrant?

How Much? How Many?

a whole watermelon

half a watermelon

a whole cake

half a cake

a full basket

an empty basket

a full pitcher

an empty pitcher

a few apples

many apples

a little ice cream

a lot of ice cream

only one cooky

a dozen cupcakes

a dozen doughnut

many cookies

a dozen eggs

112

one shoe

a pair of shoes

a pair of mittens

a pair of gloves

a dollar

a half dollar

a dime

a quarter

a nickel

a penny

There is something
in the box.

There is nothing
in the box.

This puppy
has all the bones.

This puppy
has none.

The blue jay
has some
acorns.

The chipmunk
has more acorns
than the blue jay.

The squirrel
has the most
acorns.

throw

bat

catch

climb

stand

sit

drink

wave

walk

jump

pull

ride

push

crawl

hop

read

Up, Down, and All Around

JoJo is climbing **up** the ladder.

JoJo is **at the top of** the ladder.

JoJo is **under** the ladder.

JoJo is going **into** the house.

He is coming **out of** the house.

He is running **away from** the house.

JoJo is walking **toward** the brook.

JoJo is going **across** the brook.

JoJo is **in** the brook.

JoJo is sitting
on a log.

JoJo is jumping
off the log.

JoJo is running
through the woods.

JoJo hears a buzzing
inside the hollow tree.

Something buzzy flies
out of the hollow tree.

JoJo is jumping
over the fence.

JoJo is going **up**
the mountain.

He is coming **down**
the mountain.

He is **at the bottom of**
the mountain.

Words That Make Pictures

a beautiful witch   an ugly witch

a good puppy   a naughty puppy

a clean pig   a dirty pig

a fat clown   a skinny clown

a happy girl   an unhappy girl

a fast animal   a slow animal

a busy elf   a lazy elf

a cheerful lady   a sad lady

a frightened boy   a brave boy

a plain dress   a fancy dress

a straight stick   **a crooked stick**   **a wet puppy**   **a dry puppy**

a young man   **an old man**   **a good apple**   **a bad apple**

smooth caterpillar   **a fuzzy caterpillar**   **a shiny pan**   **a dull pan**

a cross dog   **a friendly dog**   **a new toy**   **an old toy**

a funny monster   **a scary monster**   **a wide ribbon**   **a narrow ribbon**

The Circus Parade

- Who is first in the parade? Who is second? Who is last?
- How many people are in the parade? How many animals? How many clowns?
- Which animal is tallest? Which is fattest? Which is smallest?
- Where is JoJo? Where are the lions? Where is the poodle?
- What is the tall clown carrying? How many balloons has he? Tell the colors.
- What is the little clown carrying? What is the drum major holding?
- Who is behind the camel? Who is on the camel? Who is in front of the camel?

- Who is between the camel and the lions' cage?
  Who is walking in front of the bear?
- Who is wearing pink and green? Who wears an orange wig?
  Who wears a tall hat?
- Which animal has spots? Which animals are brown?
  Which two animals are alike?
- Who looks happy? Who looks sad? Who is upside down?
  Who is waving?
- How many are walking? How many are riding?
  How many have four legs?

Rhyme Time

a fish in a dish

a man in a pan

a snake eating cake

a bear with a pear

a fly on a pie

an ape in a cape

a raccoon with a spoon

a goat in a coat

a bat with a hat

a ghost eating toast

an elf on a shelf

a hen in a pen

a bee on a tree

a bunny eating honey

a clown falling down

a parrot with a carrot

a mouse in a blouse

an owl with a towel

a boy with a toy

a clock on a rock

a crow with a hoe

a sheep in a jeep

a seal on a wheel

a bug on a mug

123

The Alphabet

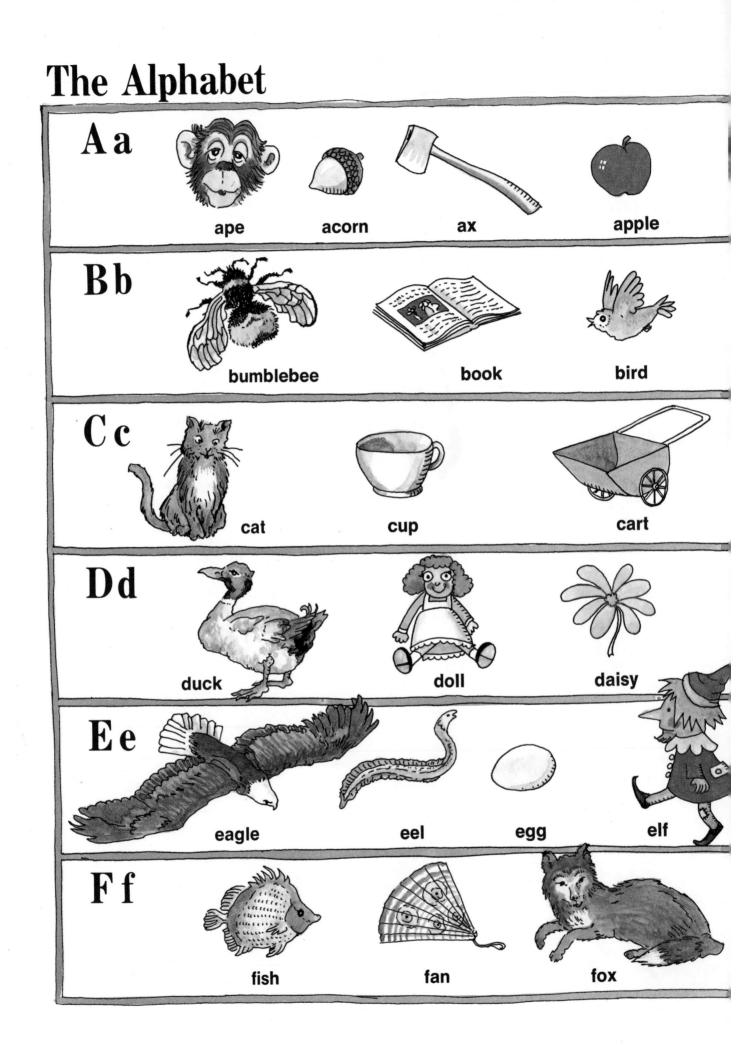

A a   ape   acorn   ax   apple

B b   bumblebee   book   bird

C c   cat   cup   cart

D d   duck   doll   daisy

E e   eagle   eel   egg   elf

F f   fish   fan   fox

Gg goat girl goose

Hh hen horn heart

Ii ice iron insect Indian

Jj jar jug jet

Kk koala king kitten

Ll lamb leaf lamp

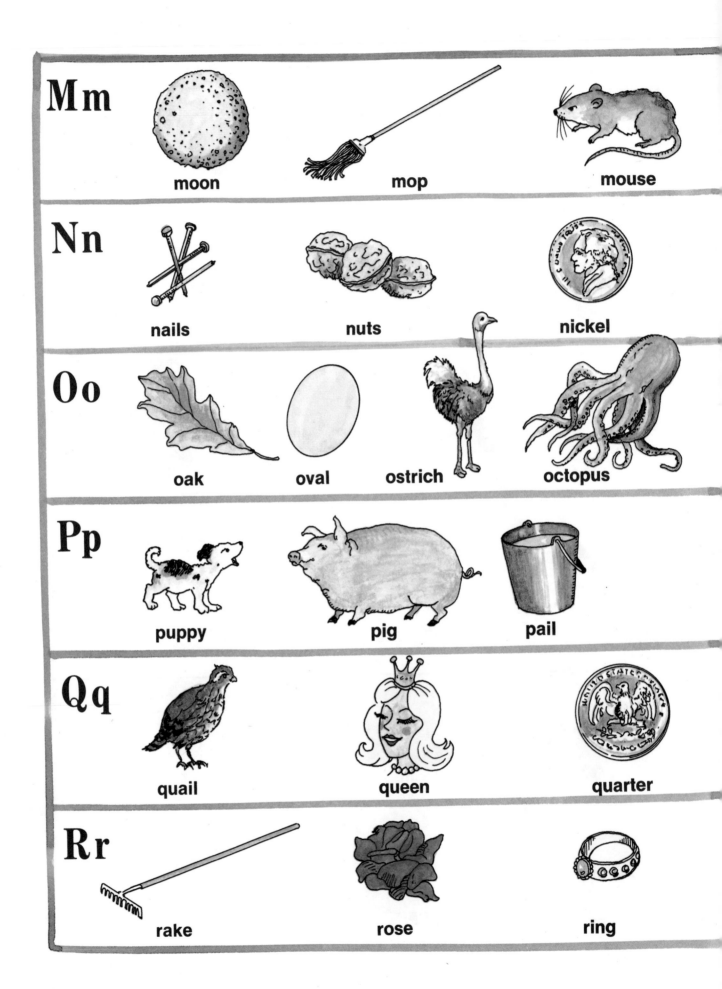

Mm

moon

mop

mouse

Nn

nails

nuts

nickel

Oo

oak

oval

ostrich

octopus

Pp

puppy

pig

pail

Qq

quail

queen

quarter

Rr

rake

rose

ring

S s

saw
sun
seal

T t

tire
turtle
tiger

U u

uniform
unicycle
umbrella
umpire

V v

violin
vase
violets

W w

watch
wolf

X x

X ray
xylophone

Y y

yak
yo-yo

Z z

zebra
zither